This book belongs to:

....

M000087353

FANTASTIC NATURE

How this collection works

This collection includes six enjoyable non-fiction texts designed to get your child thinking about the wonders of the natural world, from animals that disguise themselves as other animals to fish that can fly! These texts are full of fascinating facts and ideas, with the same high-quality artwork and photos you would expect from any non-fiction book – but they are specially written so that your child can read them for themselves. They are carefully levelled and in line with your child's phonics learning at school.

It's very important for your child to have access to non-fiction as well as stories while they are learning to read. This helps them develop a wider range of reading skills, and prepares them for learning through reading. Most children love finding out about the world as they read – and some children prefer non-fiction to story books, so it's doubly important to make sure that they have opportunities to read both.

How to use this book

Reading should be a shared and enjoyable experience for both you and your child. Pick a time when your child isn't distracted by other things, and when they are happy to concentrate for about 10 to 15 minutes. Choose one or two of the non-fiction texts for each session, so that they don't get too tired. Read the tips on the next page, as they offer ideas and suggestions for getting the most out of this collection.

Tips for reading non-fiction

STEP 1

Before your child begins reading one of the non-fiction texts, look together at the contents page for that particular text. What does your child think the text will be about? Do they know anything about this subject already? Briefly talk about your child's ideas, and remind them of anything they know about the topic if necessary. Look at the topic words and other notes for each text, and use the 'before reading' suggestions to help introduce the text to your child.

STEP 2

Point out some of the non-fiction features in the text – for example, the contents page, labelled pictures, photographs, index and glossary. Talk about how the contents page and index helps you find the different parts of the text, and the photographs help show that this is a book about the real world rather than a story.

STEP 3

Ask your child to read the text aloud. Encourage them to stop and look at the pictures, and talk about what they are reading either during the reading session, or afterwards. Your child will be able to read most of the words in the text, but if they struggle with a word, remind them to say the sounds in the word from left to right and then blend the sounds together to read the whole word, e.g. *f-l-ow-er, flower*. If they have real difficulty, tell them the word and move on.

STEP 4

When your child has finished reading, talk about what they have found out. Which bits of the text did they like most, and why? Encourage your child to do some of the fun activities that follow each text.

CONTENTS

Animal Tricks.................................7

Fantastic Plants and Animals...25

Tree Town 41

Bird Sounds................................57

Can Fish Fly? 73

Ants 89

OXFORD
UNIVERSITY PRESS

Animal Tricks

Some wild animals use tricks to hide or find food. This text looks at how different animals use camouflage to survive.

Before reading

Talk about how animals sometimes hide from their enemies by using a disguise. Explain that some animals can look like a different creature, to fool their enemies.

Topic words

These words may be challenging to read but they are important for the topic. Read them together and talk about what they mean.

bird – an animal that has wings and feathers

snake – a long reptile with scales

antenna – a long, thin feeler on an insect's head

octopus – a sea creature with eight arms (tentacles)

butterfly – an insect with a thin body and two pairs of large wings

Tricky words

These words are common but your child might find them difficult to read:

what, like, so, little, have, do

ANIMAL TRICKS

CONTENTS

Is it a Tree?......................9

Is it a Snake?..................11

Is it a Fish?..................13

Is it a Flower?..............15

Is it an Owl?...............17

What is it? 19

Glossary and Index.......22

Jan Burchett and Sara Vogler

Is it a Tree?

What is it?
Is it a tree?

No, it's a trick!
It is a bird.

It looks like a tree so
attackers cannot see it.

Is it a Snake?

What is it? Is it a snake?

No, it's a trick! It is a moth. Its **wing tips** help to frighten its attackers.

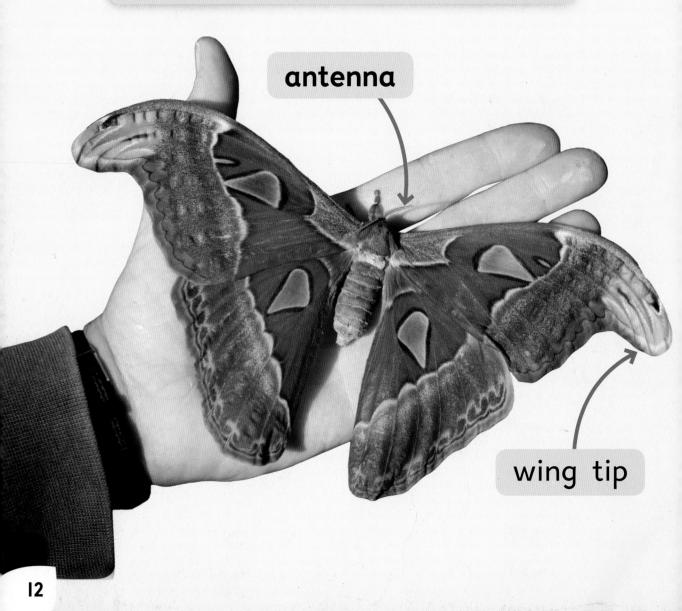

antenna

wing tip

Is it a Fish?

What is it? Is it a fish?

No, it's a trick! It is an octopus.

It's pretending to be a fish
that can hurt attackers.

Is it a Flower?

What is it?
Is it a flower?

No, it's a trick! This is a mantis. It is an **insect**.

six legs

Little insects think the mantis is a flower and land on it. The mantis feeds on little insects.

Is it an Owl?

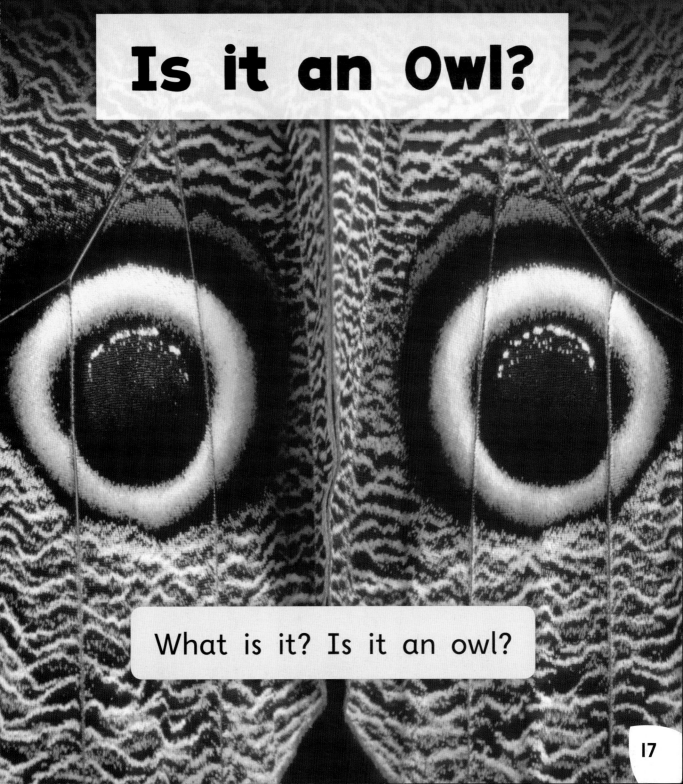

What is it? Is it an owl?

No, it's a trick! It is a butterfly.
Attackers think it's an owl.
This frightens them off.

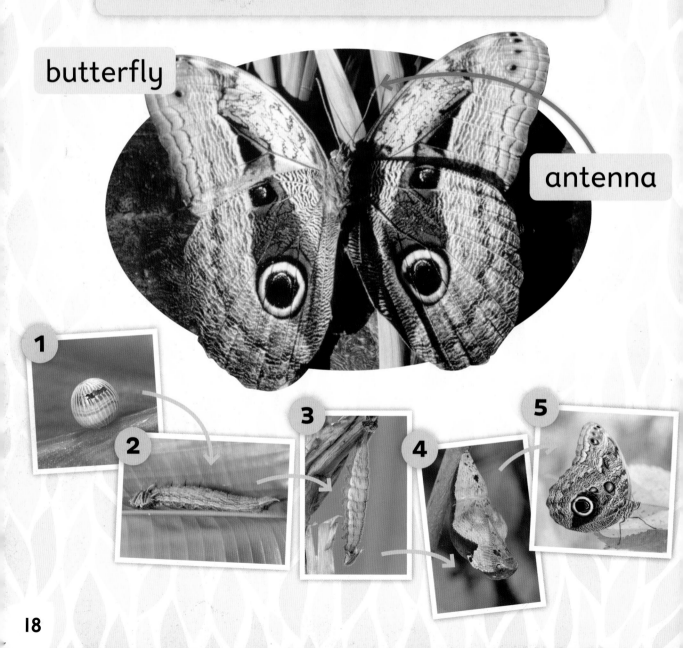

butterfly

antenna

1

2

3

4

5

What is it?

Is it a fish?
Or is it a trick?

It's not a trick! It is a shark. A shark is a big fish.

Sharks have big, sharp teeth so they do not need tricks!

I need **my** dinner!

sharp teeth

21

Glossary

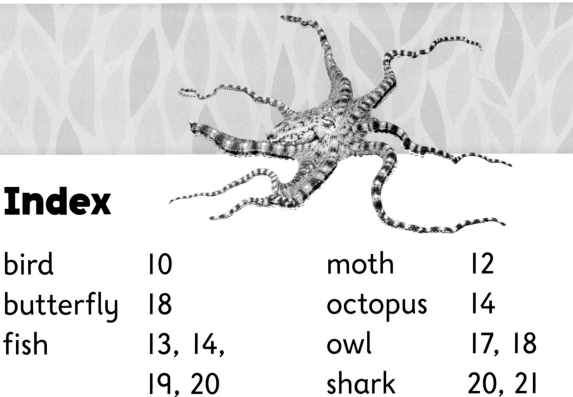

antenna: a thin feeler on an insect

insect: a little animal with six legs

wing tips: the ends of an animal's wings

Index

bird	10	moth	12
butterfly	18	octopus	14
fish	13, 14, 19, 20	owl	17, 18
		shark	20, 21
insect	16	snake	11

Talk about it!

Which animal can look like a snake? Why is this an important trick?

Match the animals

Follow the lines to match the animals with the names of the things they look like.

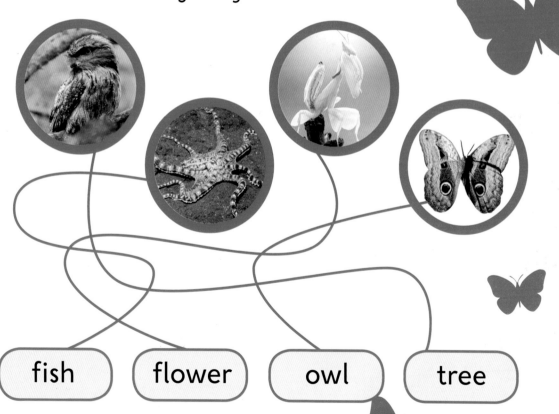

fish   flower   owl   tree

Fantastic Plants and Animals

This text compares some of the world's most amazing plants and animals – from the biggest to the smelliest!

Before reading

Does your child have a favourite plant or animal? Encourage them to talk about why it is their favourite.

Topic words

These words may be challenging to read but they are important for the topic. Read them together and talk about what they mean.

plant – a living thing that grows in soil

tall – very high

whale – a very large sea animal

orchid – a type of colourful flower

flamingo – a large bird with long legs, a long neck and pink feathers

Tricky words

These words are common but your child might find them difficult to read:

what, like, so, do

FANTASTIC PLANTS AND ANIMALS

CONTENTS

What a Stink! 26

Big and Tall 28

Odd Lookers! 30

Snack Attack! 32

Look Again 34

Bright Sight 36

Glossary and Index 38

Catherine Veitch

What a Stink!

A stink bug is an insect. It lets off a bad smell if an animal **attacks** it.

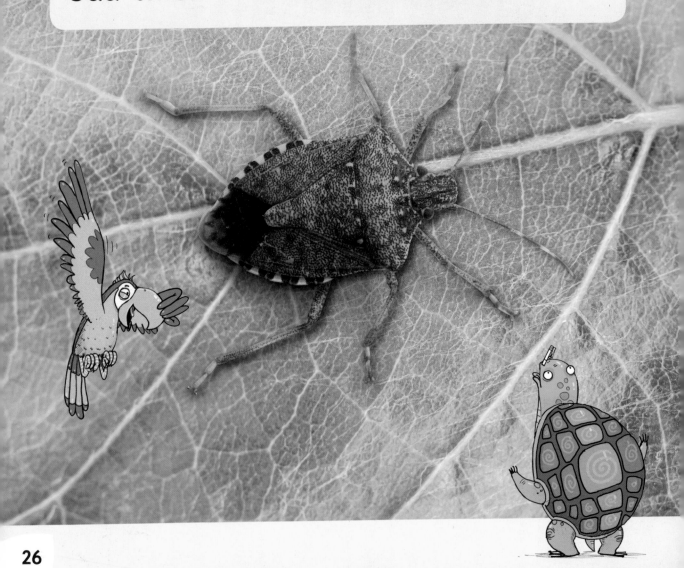

The flower on this plant smells bad! Its strong smell **attracts** insects.

starfish flower

petals

Big and Tall

This whale is the biggest animal ever!
It feeds on krill.
It needs a lot!

krill

The redwood is the tallest tree!

redwood

29

Odd Lookers!

If an animal attacks this black rain frog it puffs up like a balloon.

bat flower

This is a plant but the flower looks like the wings of a bat.

bat

Snack Attack!

This shark bumps into its food. Then it grabs the food with its sharp teeth.

Insects like the sweet smell of this plant.

The plant traps insects in its cup for food.

insect

cup

trapping plant

Look Again ...

stick insect

Animals think this stick insect is a twig, so do not **hunt** it.

Bees think this orchid is a bee and they are attracted to it.

orchid

bee

Bright Sight

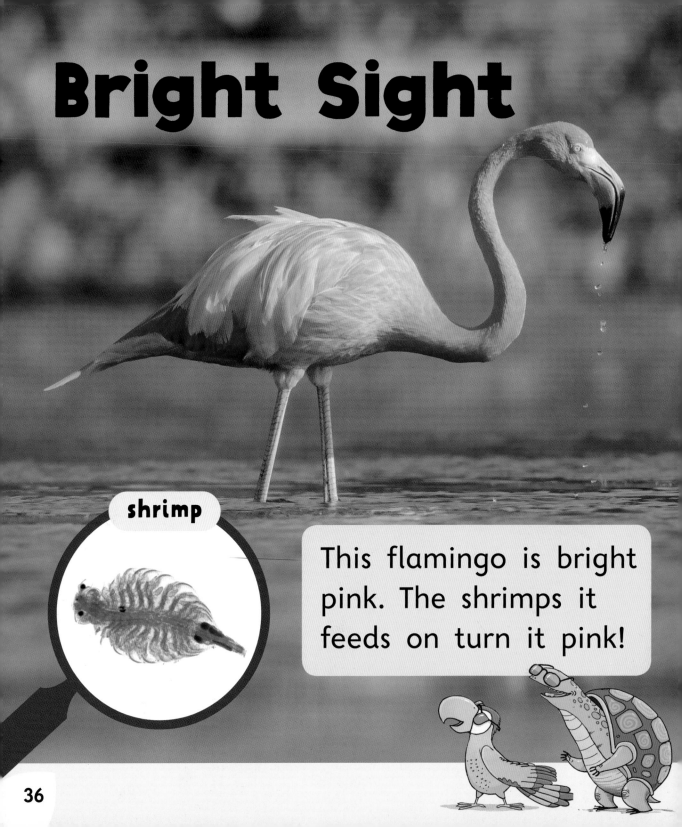

shrimp

This flamingo is bright pink. The shrimps it feeds on turn it pink!

This dragon tree has red **sap**.
It looks like it is bleeding!

bark

red sap

Glossary

attacks: hurts or fights

attracts: gets insects or animals to
 want to be near

hunt: kill for food

sap: liquid in a plant

Index

Animals		Plants	
black rain frog	30	bat flower	31
flamingo	36	dragon tree	37
shark	32	orchid	35
stick insect	34	redwood	29
stink bug	26	starfish flower	27
whale	28	trapping plant	33

Talk about it!

Which plant do you think is the most fantastic? Why?

Who gets the medals?

Award the medals to the plants you think deserve them.

| Stinky plant | Stinky animal | Big animal | Bright animal |

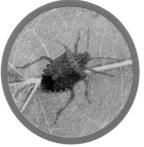

Tree Town

This text looks at all the different parts of a tree from the roots to the treetops, and introduces some of the animals who live there.

Before reading

Can your child think of any birds or animals that live in trees?

Topic words

These words may be challenging to read but they are important for the topic. Read them together and talk about what they mean.

lives – makes a home

plants – living things that grow in soil, like grass, trees or vegetables

leaves – flat green parts of a plant that grow from its stem

nectar – sweet liquid found inside flowers

treecreeper – a type of small bird

Tricky words

These words are common but your child might find them difficult to read:

what, so, have, like

TREE TOWN

CONTENTS

Tree Roots 42

Tree Trunk 44

Leaves 46

Catkins 48

Nest 50

Tree Town 52

Glossary and Index 54

Hawys Morgan

Tree Roots

den

fox cub

roots

Tree roots are strong. Roots can drink from the wet soil.

The fox digs a den in the roots.

Fox

Lives in: roots
Food: plants, animals, insects

Tree Trunk

moss

The trunk has hard bark on it.

fungus

44

Earwig

Lives in: bark, logs, leaves
Food: insects, plants

six legs →

I will put
the earwig back
on the tree!

45

Leaves

caterpillar

eggs

Look at the caterpillar
eggs on the leaf.

The leaves are food for insects and animals.

What will the caterpillar turn into?

Caterpillar

Lives in: leaves
Food: leaves!

stem

Catkins

moth

catkin

Catkins are flowers on a tree.

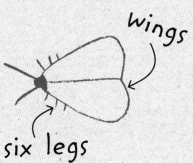

Moth

Lives in: tree
Food: nectar

wings

six legs

catkin

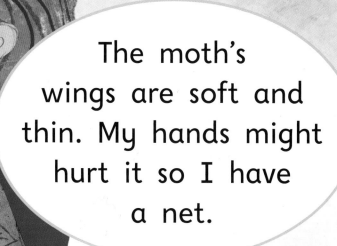

The moth's wings are soft and thin. My hands might hurt it so I have a net.

49

Nest

treecreeper

chicks

nest

twigs

moss

Treecreepers nest in the bark. They look for food in the tree for the chicks.

Treecreeper

Lives in: trees
Food: nuts, seeds, insects

51

Tree Town

leaves

treetop

Glossary

fungus: a plant with no leaves or flowers, such as a mushroom

nectar: a sweet liquid from flowers

Index

caterpillar 46, 47

catkins..........48, 49

chicks 50

den...............42, 43

earwig..........45

fox...............42, 43

moth 48, 49

nest 50

treecreeper ..50, 51

Talk about it!

Which of the creatures in the text would you like to spot in a tree? Why?

Letter scramble

Unscramble the letters to make the animal names.

p r er t ee r ee c

ar t er c i p a ll

w ear g i

x o f

Bird Sounds

This book looks at the calls and sounds of lots of amazing birds. Learn interesting facts about each bird and the very different sounds they make.

Before reading

How many different birds can your child think of? Do they know what any of these birds sound like?

Topic words

These words may be challenging to read but they are important for the topic. Read them together and talk about what they mean.

nocturnal – animals or birds that sleep during the day and are active at night

attract – to interest someone or something

lyrebird – a rainforest bird with a long tail

rainforest – a tropical forest where it rains a lot

chainsaws – big saws with motors

Tricky words

These words are common but your child might find them difficult to read:

called, their, people

BIRD SOUNDS

CONTENTS

Diver 58

Mallard Duck 59

Tawny Owl 60

Barking Owl 61

Geese 62

Falcon 64

Cuckoo 66

Kookaburra 67

Yellowhammer 68

Lyrebird 69

Glossary and Index 70

Mick Manning

Diver

Birds make all sorts of sounds.
Some birds sing songs and other
birds just make loud noises!

This diver bird is calling
across a lake.

Wheeoooo-oo!
Wheeoooo-oo-oop!

The diver is also called a 'loon'.
Divers live in many parts of the world.

Mallard Duck

This mother duck calls
to her ducklings.

Quack-quack-quack!

Mallard ducks have about 12 fluffy ducklings.

Tawny Owl

Some owls hoot! One tawny owl calls "Too-wit," then another replies "Hoo-hoo."

Too-wit!

Hoo-hoo!

Tawny owls are nocturnal. This means they sleep in the day and are awake at night.

Barking Owl

Not all owls hoot.
This owl sounds a
bit like a dog barking.

Woof! Woof!

Barking owls live in Australia. They
eat mice, birds and even rabbits.

Geese

These birds call out as they fly.

Honk-honk!

Honk-honk!

Honk-honk!

Honk-honk!

Geese need to keep together when they fly. When they call out it helps them to find each other.

Falcon

This falcon is calling to scare away a crow from her nest.

Falcons nest on cliffs. They also nest on tall buildings in some cities.

Keck-keck-keck!

Cuckoo

This **male** cuckoo is singing to **attract** a **female**. Only male cuckoos sing this sort of song.

Cuckoo-cuckoo!

Female cuckoos lay their eggs in other birds' nests. This tricks the other birds into looking after the cuckoo's eggs.

Kookaburra

The kookaburra is a noisy bird. Its song sounds like someone laughing!

Kook-kook-ar-ar-ar-bra!

Kookaburras live in Australia. They eat lizards, mice and small birds.

Yellowhammer

This bird sings in a pattern
that can sound like words.

A little bit of bread and no cheese!

Yellowhammers lay
eggs that have
wonderful patterns.
Each egg is different.

Lyrebird

This bird can copy the sounds it hears.

Brum-brum-brrrrrr-bzzzz!
Kerching-kerching!
Whizzzzzz!

Lyrebirds live in the **rainforest**. Sometimes people cut down the trees using **chainsaws**. The lyrebirds can copy the *sound* of the chainsaws.

Glossary

attract: to interest another bird

chainsaw: a saw with a motor for cutting down trees

female: girl

male: boy

rainforest: a tropical forest where it rains a lot

Index

call	58, 59, 60, 62, 63, 64
fly	62, 63
live	58, 61, 67, 69
nest	64, 66
sing	58, 66, 68

Talk about it!

What kind of tool can I sound like? Why do I make this sound?

Word search

Find the bird names in the word search.

w	c	f	f	a	l	c	o	n	b
r	u	r	q	a	y	n	v	s	c
c	c	v	b	b	r	j	k	l	l
z	k	w	s	f	e	n	b	d	r
k	o	o	k	a	b	u	r	r	a
a	o	w	a	s	i	w	c	t	t
b	m	l	p	e	r	i	o	u	y
g	e	e	s	e	d	u	c	k	w

lyrebird

owl

cuckoo

kookaburra

falcon

geese

duck

Can Fish Fly?

This text is a true or false quiz about surprising animal facts. Find out the answer to each question, plus more details about the animal's amazing abilities!

Before reading

Talk about the title with your child. Do they think there could be a type of fish that can fly?

Topic words

These words may be challenging to read but they are important for the topic. Read them together and talk about what they mean.

taste – find out the flavour of something

hippopotamus – a large African animal that spends a lot of time in water

sunscreen – cream to stop skin from getting sunburnt

sweats – when liquid comes out of skin when it is hot

glides – moves smoothly through the air

Tricky words

This word is common but your child might find it difficult to read:

their

CAN FISH FLY?

CONTENTS

Octopus Brains................. 75

Camel Humps 77

Hippopotamus Skin........ 79

Butterfly Feet................. 81

Fish Fins 83

Glossary and Index...... 86

Rob Alcraft

Get ready for some fantastic facts!
But are they true or are they false?
Can you decide?

True or false?

An octopus has nine **brains**.
Is it true? What do you think?

Find out this way!

It's true! An octopus has one brain in its body and eight little brains in its arms.

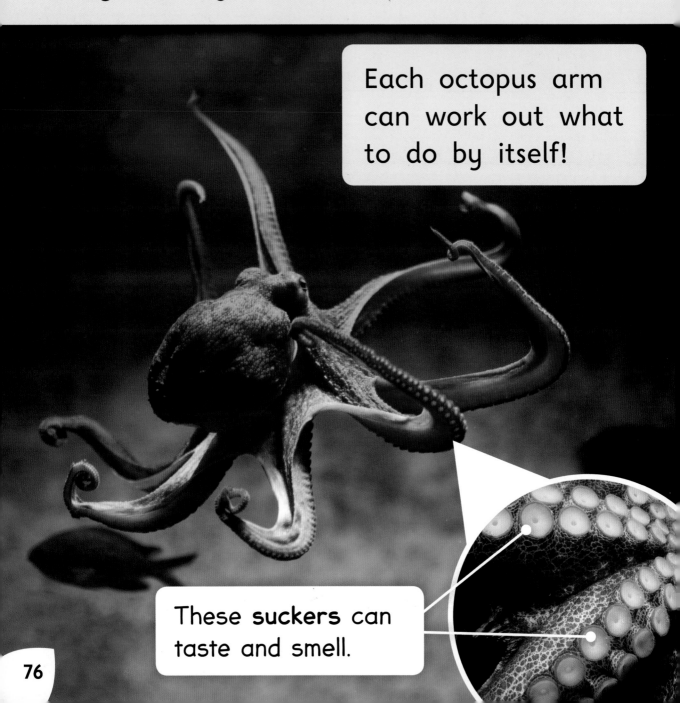

Each octopus arm can work out what to do by itself!

These **suckers** can taste and smell.

True or false?

Camels store drinking water in their humps.
Can it be true?

It's false! Camels don't store drinking water in their humps. They store fat.

The fat in the humps keeps the camel alive when there is no food.

As the fat gets used up, the camel's humps go floppy!

True or false?

A hippopotamus makes its own **sunscreen**.
That can't be true ... or can it?

It's true! Hippopotamuses make their own sunscreen. It is red and it **sweats** out through their skin.

Hippopotamuses like being in water. It keeps them cool.

True or false?

Butterflies taste with their feet.
Can that be true?

It's true! Butterflies use their feet to taste for food! They feed on the juice of fruit and flowers.

This rolled-up tube is part of the butterfly's mouth. It works like a long straw.

True or false?

There is a fish that can fly.

Is that really true?

It's true ... well, sort of! The flying fish leaps out of the sea and **glides** a long way over the waves.

Lots of bigger animals want to eat flying fish. Gliding helps them to get away.

Flying fish use their long fins like wings to glide.

Animals are amazing! There's even a flying fish. Now you know!

Glossary

brains: parts that allow us to think and control our bodies

glides: travels through the air very smoothly

suckers: parts of an animal's body that help it to cling on

sunscreen: a liquid that you put on skin to protect it from the sun

sweats: when liquid comes out of skin when it is hot

Index

brains	75, 76	suckers	76
feet	81, 82	sunscreen	79, 80
fins	85	taste	76, 81, 82
humps	77, 78	wings	85

Talk about it!

Could you get a nice drink of water from my hump? Why?

What am I?

Read the clues to find out which animals are being described.

1. I have nine brains.

2. I make my own sunscreen.

3. I taste with my feet.

4. I can glide over the waves.

Answers: 1. octopus; 2. hippopotamus; 3. butterfly; 4. flying fish

Ants

Join Sam and his big brother as they find out all about ants – where they live, what they eat, and their life cycle.

Before reading

Has your child ever watched ants crawling about in the garden or park? What are ants like, and what do they do?

Topic words

These words may be challenging to read but they are important for the topic. Read them together and talk about what they mean.

antennae – long, thin feelers on an insect's head

colony – a group of animals that live and work together

larvae – tiny animals that hatch out of eggs and grow into insects

soldier – soldier ants look after the ant nest and keep it safe from threats and enemies

cocoons – coverings that protect baby insects while they grow into adults

Tricky words

These words are common but your child might find them difficult to read:

called, asked, looked, could, people

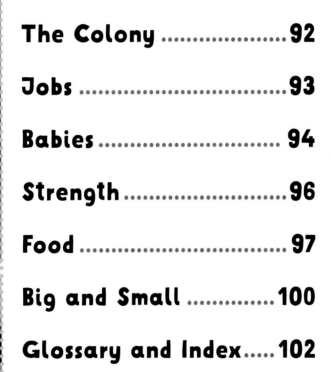

ANTS

CONTENTS

The Colony 92

Jobs 93

Babies 94

Strength 96

Food 97

Big and Small 100

Glossary and Index 102

Vivian French

My little brother Sam loved watching ants.

"Look!" Sam said. "Beetles!"

"Those are ants," I said. "Ants are clever."

"Why?" Sam asked.

"Can you see those feelers on its head?"
I said. "Those are **antennae**. Ants use them
to tell each other about food and danger!"

"Ants look after each other," I said. "They live in a group, just like a big family! The group is called a **colony**."

"What do they all do?" Sam asked.

"The queen ant lays eggs," I told him. "The worker ants collect food. The soldier ants look after the colony."

Sam looked at my picture.
"What are ant babies like?" he asked.

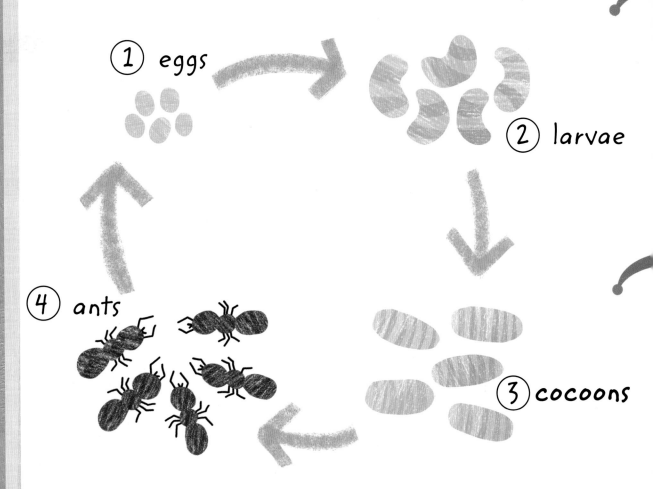

1 eggs
2 larvae
3 cocoons
4 ants

"First, the queen lays some eggs,"
I told him. "The eggs hatch into
larvae. Then the larvae make cocoons
and turn into ants."

"Tell me about the soldier ants," said Sam. "Do they fight?"

"Yes," I said. "Sometimes they fight the ants from another colony."

Go away!

"Did you know that ants are very strong?" I asked. "If Dad was as strong as an ant, he could carry a car!"

"What do ants eat?" Sam asked.
He liked eating.

"They eat almost anything!" I said.
"They like fruit, seeds and dead bugs.
And they love sugar!"

Yum! Lovely cake!

Sam frowned. "They might eat my cake!" he said.

98

"Well, people eat ants in some parts of the world!" I said.

Tasty roasted ants!

I pointed at an ant. "Look how tiny it is. The biggest ants are longer than your thumb! They live in South America."

There are more than 12 000 different sorts of ant.

smallest =
1 millimetre

largest =
30 millimetres

Sam let an ant crawl over his hand.
"I love ants ..." he said.

"That's good," I said. "Because there
are lots and lots and lots
of ants in the world!"

Glossary

antennae: long, thin feelers on an insect's head

cocoons: coverings that protect baby insects while they change into adults

colony: a group of animals that live and work together

larvae: tiny animals that hatch out of eggs and turn into insects

millimetre: a way of measuring how long something is

Index

antennae.. 91, 93

cocoons.... 94

colony...... 92, 93, 95

eggs 92, 93, 94

food 91, 93, 97–99

larvae....... 92, 94

queen....... 92, 93, 94

soldiers..... 93, 95

workers 92, 93

Talk about it!

Which sort of ant would you rather be – worker, soldier or queen? Why?

Maze

Help the ant to reach the cake!

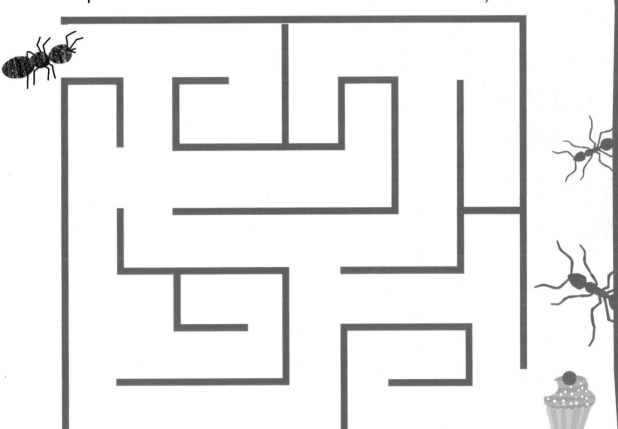

OXFORD
UNIVERSITY PRESS

Great Clarendon Street, Oxford, OX2 6DP, United Kingdom

Oxford University Press is a department of the University of Oxford. It furthers the University's objective of excellence in research, scholarship, and education by publishing worldwide. Oxford is a registered trade mark of Oxford University Press in the UK and in certain other countries

Animal Tricks text © Jan Burchett and Sara Vogler 2016

Fantastic Plants and Animals text © Catherine Veitch 2016
Illustrations © Aleksei Bitskoff 2016

Tree Town text © Hawys Morgan 2016
Illustrations © Frann Preston-Gannon 2016

Birds Sounds text © Mick Manning and Brita Granstrom 2016
Illustrations © Mick Manning 2016

Can Fish Fly? text © Rob Alcraft 2016
Illustrations © Mark Beech 2016

Ants text © Vivian French 2016
Illustrations © Madison Mastrangelo 2016

The moral rights of the authors have been asserted

This Edition published in 2019

All rights reserved. No part of this publication may be reproduced, stored in a retrieval system, or transmitted, in any form or by any means, without the prior permission in writing of Oxford University Press, or as expressly permitted by law, by licence or under terms agreed with the appropriate reprographics rights organization. Enquiries concerning reproduction outside the scope of the above should be sent to the Rights Department, Oxford University Press, at the address above.

You must not circulate this work in any other form and you must impose this same condition on any acquirer

British Library Cataloguing in Publication Data
Data available

ISBN: 978-0-19-276969-5

10 9 8 7 6 5 4 3 2 1

Paper used in the production of this book is a natural, recyclable product made from wood grown in sustainable forests. The manufacturing process conforms to the environmental regulations of the country of origin.

Printed in China

Acknowledgements

Series Editor: Nikki Gamble

Animal Tricks

The publisher would like to thank the following for permission to reproduce photographs: **p9:** Mjarnold87/Dreamstime; **p10:** Craig Dingle/Istockphoto; **p11:** Vladimir Sazonov/Shutterstock; **p12:** Joel Sartore/Getty Images; **p12, p14, p18** and **p22:** Shutterstock; **p13:** Aquanaut4/Dreamstime.com; **p14** and **p22:** Georgette Douwma/ Nature Picture Library; **p15:** Roger Meets/Shutterstock; **p16:** kuritafsheen/Getty Images; Shutterstock; **p17:** Danita Delimont/Alamy; Buddy Mays/Corbis; Kim Taylor/Getty Images; **p18:** Survivalphotos; WILDLIFE GmbH; John Cancalosi/Nature Picture Library; Ogphoto/ Istockphoto; **p19:** Jennifer Hayes/Getty Images; **p20:** Tolga TEZCAN/ Istockphoto; **p21:** Denis Scott/Fuse/Getty Images; **p22:** Mathisa/ Shutterstock

Fantastic Plants and Animals

The publisher would like to thank the following for permission to reproduce photographs: **p26:** Mete Uz/Alamy; Shutterstock; **p27:** Hal Horwitz/Corbis; **p28:** Franco Banf/Nature Picture Library; David Tipling/ Nature Picture Library; **p29:** franckreporter/ Getty Images; **p30:** Photoshot License Ltd/Alamy; **p31:** Mauritius Images GmbH; Nature Photographers Ltd/Alamy; **p32:** Jim Abernethy/Getty Images; **p33** and **p35:** Claude Nuridsany & Marie Perennou/Science Photo Library; **p34:** blickwinkel/Alamy; **p35:** 271700615/Shutterstock; Paulrommer/Shutterstock; **p36:** Getty Images; Dr Keith Wheeler/ Science Photo Library; **p37:** Alex7370/Shutterstock; Dr Morley Read/ Science Photo Library

Tree Town

All photography by Shutterstock

Can Fish Fly?

The publisher would like to thank the following for permission to reproduce photographs: **p76:** Shutterstock; Jeff Rotman/Alamy Stock Photo; **p78:** Shutterstock; **p80:** Anup Shah/naturepl; Ariadne Van Zandbergen/Alamy Stock Photo; **p82:** tcp/Istockphoto; **p84:** Nature Picture Library/Alamy Stock Photo; **p84** and **p85:** WILDLIFE GmbH/ Alamy Stock Photo.

Ants

The publisher would like to thank the following for permission to reproduce photographs: **p89:** Redmond Durrell/Alamy Stock Photo; all other images by Shutterstock.

All other images Shutterstock

Cover images Shutterstock